H

D1444815

# The Life Cycle of a

# STICKLEBACK

Philip Parker

Illustrated by
## Jackie Harland

Reading Consultant:
## Diana Bentley

**The Bookwright Press**
**New York · 1988**

# Life Cycles

The Life Cycle of an Ant
The Life Cycle of a Butterfly
The Life Cycle of a Frog
The Life Cycle of a Rabbit
The Life Cycle of a Stickleback
The Life Cycle of a Sunflower

First published in the
United States in 1988 by
The Bookwright Press
387 Park Avenue South
New York, NY 10016

First published in 1988 by
Wayland (Publishers) Limited
61 Western Road, Hove
East Sussex, BN3 1JD, England

**Library of Congress Cataloging-in-Publication Data**
Parker, Philip
  Life cycle of a stickleback/by Philip Parker.
    p.   cm. – (Life cycles)
  Bibliography: p.
  Includes index.
  ISBN 0-531-18190-1
  1. Three-spined stickleback—Juvenile literature.
  I. Title   II. Series
QL638.G27P37 1988
597′.53—dc 19                                    87–33759
                                                        CIP
                                                         AC

Typeset in the UK by DP Press Limited, Sevenoaks, Kent
Printed by Casterman S.A., Belgium

**Notes for parents and teachers**
Each title in this series has been specially written and
designed as a first natural history book for young readers.
For less able readers there are introductory captions,
while the more detailed text explains each illustration.

# Contents

Three-spined sticklebacks                    4
Sticklebacks live in ponds and streams       7
The male changes color                       8
The male dances for the female              11
The female goes into the nest               12
The female lays her eggs                    15
The male swims through the nest             16
The male looks after the eggs               19
The young come out of the eggs              20
The young hide in the weeds                 23
The young are on their own                  24
Full-grown sticklebacks                     27
Having your own fish                        28
The life cycle                              30
Glossary                                    31
Finding out more                            32
Index                                       32

All the words that are
in **bold** are explained in
the glossary on page 31.

# Three-spined stickleback fish.

These fish are called three-spined sticklebacks. Can you see why they are called three-spined? Look at their backs, they have three spikes on them. There are many different kinds of sticklebacks and they get their name from the number of **spines** they have.

# Sticklebacks live in ponds and streams.

Three-spined sticklebacks live in ponds and streams but some can live in the ocean. They are small fish, only about the size of your finger. They live together in very large groups. Each group is called a **shoal**.

# The male changes color and builds a nest.

Springtime is the **breeding season** for three-spined sticklebacks. The males leave the shoal to make their nests. The male's belly and throat turn red and his eyes turn blue. Each male builds his nest from water weeds, making sure that there is a tunnel large enough for females to swim through.

# The male stickleback dances for the female.

A female three-spined stickleback comes to the male's nest. See how her belly is swollen with eggs. The male sees that she is ready to lay her eggs, so he does not chase her away. He dances a zig-zag dance for her.

# The female stickleback goes inside the nest.

After the dance, the female stickleback follows the male to the nest. He pokes his head into the tunnel to show her how to enter the nest. The nest is not very wide, so the female has to squeeze into the tunnel.

# The female stickleback lays her eggs.

Now she is in the nest. Can you see the male? He is tickling her tail with his **snout**. This makes her lay about a hundred eggs. As soon as the last egg is laid, she leaves the nest and swims away. Often, more than one female will come to lay eggs in the same nest.

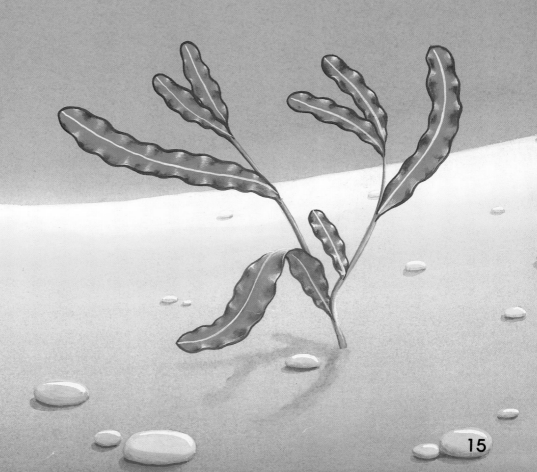

# The male stickleback swims through the nest.

Now the male swims through the nest. As he swims over the eggs he sprays them with a liquid from his body. This liquid is called **sperm**. The eggs have now been **fertilized**. Without the male's sperm, the stickleback eggs would not be able to grow.

# The male stickleback looks after the eggs.

The male stickleback looks after the fertilized eggs. He uses his **fins** to fan water over them, which keeps the eggs fresh and keeps them from being eaten by enemies. He will look after the eggs in this way for one to two weeks.

# The young come out of their eggs.

After five days you can see the black eyes and tail of each new three-spined stickleback inside the eggs. When they are this young they are called **embryos**. When they are nine days old the young fish will wriggle until they **hatch** out of their jelly-like eggs.

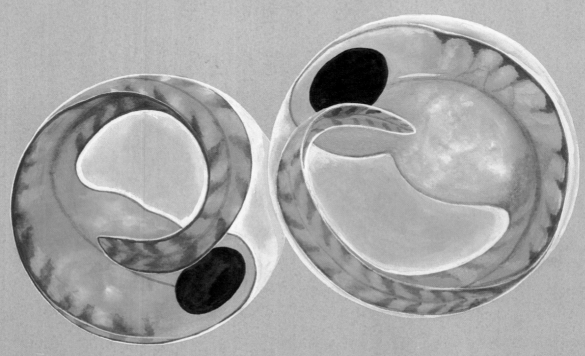

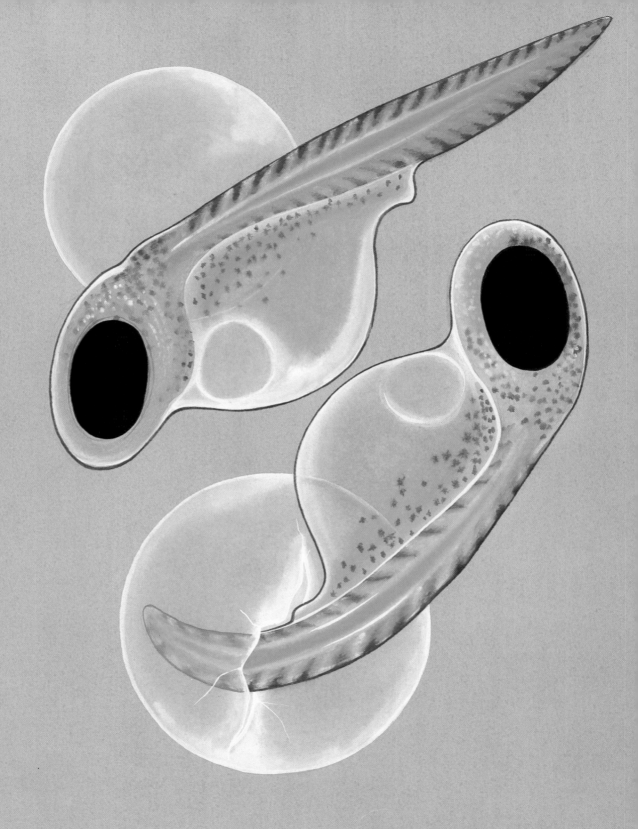

# The young fish hide in the weeds.

For the first few days the young fish hide in the weeds to escape from enemies such as larger fish and **water beetles**. The male stays to look after as many of them as he can.

# The young sticklebacks are on their own.

It is four weeks since the fish hatched out of their eggs. The bright colors of their father have faded and he swims away. He leaves the young fish to look after themselves. Can you see the bright blue bird? He is called a **kingfisher**. He likes to eat young stickleback fish.

# Full-grown three-spined sticklebacks.

The young three-spined sticklebacks eat lots of different things such as **water fleas, shrimp** and worms. When they are full-grown they will be as long as your finger. Next spring each male will build his own nest. What do you think will happen then?

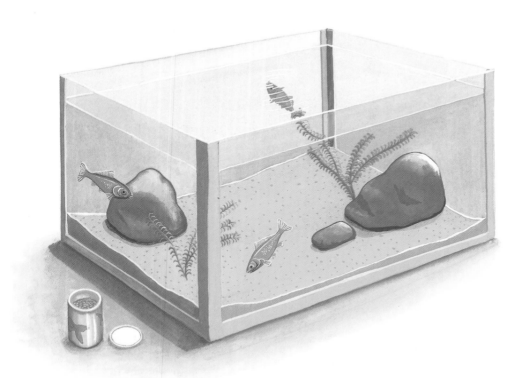

# Having your own fish.

Sticklebacks cannot normally be bought in pet shops because they do not make good pets. If you would like to have your own fish, goldfish are easy to look after. They must be kept in a fish tank or a fish bowl. Wash some small stones and put a layer in the bottom of the tank. Add some water weeds and wrap their ends around the stones.

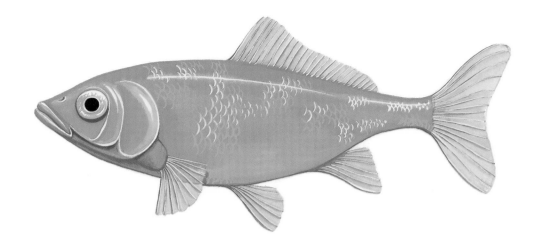

Slowly fill the tank with water and leave
it to settle for two days. Now you can put
the fish carefully into the water. Feed
your goldfish on a very small amount of
dried fish food, bought from a pet shop.
It is very important to keep the water
clean. When the water starts to look
dirty, fill a jar with clean water and
leave it to settle for two hours. Carefully
put the fish into the jar. Clean out the
tank and rinse the stones well. Fill the
tank with clean water. Leave the water
to settle for two hours. Now you can put
your fish back into their tank.

# The life cycle of a stickleback.

How many stages of the life cycle of a stickleback can you remember?

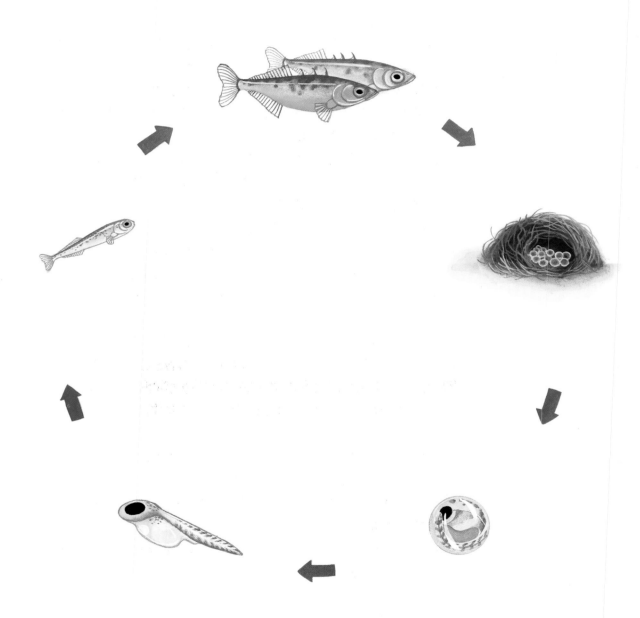

# Glossary

**Breeding season**  The time of the year when animals begin to make their young. Each kind of animal has its own breeding season.

**Embryos**  When the young are still inside the eggs we call them embryos.

**Fertilized**  When the eggs have been mixed with **sperm** and begin to grow, they have been fertilized.

**Fins**  Parts that stick out from the body of a fish. They help fish to swim and steer through the water.

**Hatch**  To break out of an egg.

**Kingfisher**  A beautiful blue and orange bird that lives near water and feeds on fish.

**Shoal**  A large group of fish that live together.

**Shrimp**  A small shellfish with a long tail that lives in ponds, streams and the ocean.

**Snout**  The mouth, nose and jaws of a fish.

**Sperm**  A liquid from the male stickleback that must mix with the eggs if they are to grow.

**Spines**  Hard, pointed spikes that grow out of the stickleback's back.

**Water beetles**  Beetles that live in rivers and ponds.

**Water fleas**  Tiny creatures that live in ponds and streams.

# Finding out more

Here are some books to read to find out more about sticklebacks and other fish.

*A Fish Hatches* by Joanna Cole (William Morrow, 1978)
*Discovering Freshwater Fish* by Bernice Brewster (Bookwrigh Press, 1988)
*The Fish Book* by Cynthia Overbeck (Lerner Publications, 19
*Fish* by Fiona Henrie (Franklin Watts, 1981)
*The Fish: The Story of the Stickleback* by Margaret Lane (Dia Books Younger, 1982)

# Index

breeding season   8

eggs   11, 15, 16, 19, 20, 24
embryos   20
enemies   19, 23, 24

females   8, 11, 12, 15
fertilization   16
fins   19
food   27

hatching   20
having fish   28-9

kingfishers   24

males   8, 11, 12, 15, 16, 19, 23, 24, 27

nests   8, 11, 12, 15, 16, 19
shoals   7, 8
snouts   15
sperm   16
spines   4

tunnels   8, 12

water beetles   23

young sticklebacks   20, 23, 24, 27